W9-CGX-291

Paleo Slow Cooker

EASY AND DELICIOUS GLUTEN-FREE
PALEO SLOW COOKER RECIPES FOR
A HEALTHY PALEO DIET

antarespress

Copyright © 2014 by Antares Press.

All rights reserved.

No part of this publication may be reproduced, stored in a retrieval system or transmitted in any form or by any means, electronic, mechanical, photocopying, recording, scanning or otherwise, except as permitted under Sections 107 or 108 of the 1976 United States Copyright Act, without the prior written permission of the Publisher.

Limit of Liability/Disclaimer of Warranty: The Publisher and the author make no representations or warranties with respect to the accuracy or completeness of the contents of this work and specifically disclaim all warranties, including without limitation warranties of fitness for a particular purpose. No warranty may be created or extended by sales or promotional materials. The advice and strategies contained herein may not be suitable for every situation. This work is sold with the understanding that the publisher is not engaged in rendering medical, legal or other professional advice or services. If professional assistance is required, the services of a competent professional person should be sought. Neither the Publisher nor the author shall be liable for damages arising herefrom. The fact that an individual, organization or website is referred to in this work as a citation and/or potential source of further information does not mean that the author or the Publisher endorses the information the individual, organization or website may provide or recommendations they/it may make. Further, readers should be aware that Internet websites listed in this work may have changed or disappeared between when this work was written and when it is read.

Antares Press publishes its books in a variety of electronic and print formats. Some content that appears in print may not be available in electronic books, and vice versa.

TRADEMARKS: Antares Press and the Antares Press logo are trademarks or registered trademarks in the United States and other countries, and may not be used without written permission. All other trademarks are the property of their respective owners. Antares Press is not associated with any product or vendor mentioned in this book.

CONTENTS

Chapter 4: Meat Dishes

Chapter 5: Vegetarian Dishes

Chapter 6: Desserts

WHAT IS "THE PALEO DIET"?

The Paleo (or Paleolithic) is more than just a diet. It's a healthy lifestyle, based on the ancestral human diet.

It has become incredibly popular in the past few years and includes various names like: Paleo(lithic) diet, Primal diet, Caveman diet, Hunter-Gatherer Diet or even the Stone Age diet.

The Paleo diet come close to the eating habits of our Paleolithic ancestors, the "hunters and gatherers"- eating foods that our bodies recognize as food (as close to their natural state as possible). Eating this way you will become leaner, meaner, and healthier.

Today we can distinguish several versions of the Paleo diet; some follow the eating patterns of our Paleolithic ancestors more strictly than other. We aim with this book to duplicate the nutritional value of a Paleolithic diet without being complicated and totally unrealistic. The Paleo diet we believe in is moderate in its approach, with great results within a reasonable period of time.

Breakfasts

SLOW COOKER BREAKFAST CAS-SEROLE

BREAKFASTS › CHORIZO SAUSAGE, ONION, EGGS, COCONUT MILK, BUTTERNUT SQUASH

1 pound nitrite-free chorizo sausage

1 small onion

12 large organic eggs

1 cup coconut milk

1 small butternut squash

ghee/oil for greasing the crockpot

In a skillet, start to cook the chorizo. Meanwhile, dice the onion.

Once the fat has begun to render, add the onion, cooking just until the onion is soft (you don't need to finish cooking the sausage — it will finish in the slow cooker).

Whip together eggs and coconut milk.

Peel, de-seed, and slice/dice/chop the squash.

Grease the inside of your slow cooker (to help minimize the sticking).

Put in the squash, the sausage/onion mixture, and then the egg/milk mixture. Stir and make sure that all of the food is covered by the egg/milk mixture.

Turn crock pot on low for 8-10 hours.

Serve.

Note: If you try another combination, you might need a little salt, pepper (in this recipe the chorizo had enough salt and other spices).

SUPER EASY CROCKPOT BREAK-FAST PIE

BREAKFASTS › EGGS, SWEET POTATO, PORK SAUSAGE, ONION, BASIL, VEGGIES

8 large organic eggs, whisked

1 sweet potato or yam, shredded

1 pound nitrite-free, uncured, pork sausage, broken up

1 yellow onion, diced

1 tablespoon garlic powder

2 teaspoons dried basil

salt and pepper, to taste

extra veggies, to taste (peppers, squash, etc.)

Grease the slow cooker with a bit of coconut oil to make sure none of the egg stuck to it.

Shred the sweet potato.

Add all ingredients to your crockpot and use a spoon to mix well.

Place on low for 6-8 hours.

Slice it like a pie.

Serve.

BREAKFAST SWEET POTATO CAS-SEROLE

BREAKFASTS › BEEF, EGGS, SWEET POTATOES, ONION, CAYENNE

2 pounds of lean ground beef

1/2 pound of bacon

8 large organic eggs

3 large sweet potatoes

1 large white onion

1 large red onion

spices: cayenne, paprika, garlic, black pepper, oregano

coconut oil

Peel the sweet potatoes and microwave for 2-3 minutes to soften them slightly.

Slice the sweet potatoes into 1/8 inch slices.

Dice the bacon finely and brown it in a pan into crisp pieces.

Remove the bacon from the pan and set it aside for later.

Dice the onions into large chunks and add to the pan along with the ground beef. Make sure you use a deep skillet or pan big enough to brown 2 pounds of beef and 2 onions.

Season the beef as you wish. Use cayenne, paprika, black pepper, garlic powder, and oregano.

Make sure the beef is fully browned and onions are translucent.

Beat eggs in a bowl, blender, or food processor. Add some cayenne and paprika to the egg mixture.

Grease the slow cooker with coconut oil.

Line the bottom of the slow cooker with slices of sweet potato. Just enough to cover the bottom.

Spoon in a layer of your seasoned beef onto the sweet potatoes.

Sprinkle some of the crisped bacon pieces on top of the beef.

Repeat.

Keep layering evenly until you use up your supplies.

Once you have finished layering, pour the egg mixture over the top.

Cook on low for 6 hours.

Allow pot to cool. You can then slice the casserole into pretty pieces.

BREAKFAST MEATLOAF

BREAKFASTS › PORK, EGGS, ONION, MAPLE SYR-
UP, FENNEL, GARLIC, OREGANO, SAGE, THYME,
PAPRIKA

1 tablespoon coconut oil

2 pounds organic pork

2 cups onions, diced

2 large, organic eggs

2 tablespoons maple syrup

1/2 cup almond flour

2 teaspoons fennel seeds

1 tablespoon garlic powder

2 teaspoons pepper flakes

2 teaspoons oregano

2 teaspoons sage

1 teaspoon sea salt

1 teaspoon paprika

1 teaspoons black pepper

2 teaspoons thyme

Soften up the diced onions in a skillet with some coconut oil.
After the onions are translucent, you can take them off the heat
and set aside.

In a bowl, add in the rest of the ingredients besides the pork and whisk them all together to combine.

Add the onions and the pork to this bowl and combine everything together again. Take this mixture and place it into the middle of the slow cooker. Shape into a loaf and place the lid on top.

Cook the meatloaf on low for around 3 hours.

Serve.

SLOW COOKED SPICED PEACHES

BREAKFASTS › PEACH, HONEY, CINNAMON, NUT-
MEG, VANILLA, COCONUT CREAM

8 peaches, peeled and sliced

1/4 cup honey

2 tablespoons coconut butter

1 teaspoon cinnamon

1/2 teaspoon nutmeg

2 teaspoons vanilla

dash of sea salt

coconut cream to pour over

Place the peaches into the slow cooker.

Pour honey, coconut butter, cinnamon, nutmeg, vanilla and sea salt over them.

Cook on high for 1 1/2 - 2 hours until peaches are tender.

Serve with coconut cream.

HAM AND SPINACH BAKE

BREAKFASTS › BABY SPINACH, HAM, MUSH-
ROOMS, GREEK YOGURT, EGGS, ONION, GARLIC

6 large organic eggs

1/2 teaspoon sea salt

1/4 teaspoon pepper

1/4 cup coconut milk

1/2 cup Greek yogurt

1/2 teaspoon thyme

1/2 teaspoon onion powder

1/2 teaspoon garlic powder

1/3 cup diced mushrooms

1 cup baby spinach (packed)

1 cup ham (diced)

1 - 2 tablespoons coconut oil

Whisk together eggs, salt, pepper, coconut milk, Greek yogurt, thyme, onion and garlic in a medium bowl until well blended. Add in ham, spinach and mushrooms.

Grease the slow cooker with coconut oil and pour in the egg mixture. Cook on high for 2 hours or until egg is fully set.

Serve warm.

BANANA PORRIDGE

BREAKFASTS › BANANA, HONEY, COCONUT MILK, CINNAMON, CLOVES, ALMONDS, SUNFLOWER SEEDS, COCONUT FLAKES

1 cup applesauce

1 banana

3/4 cup almond meal

5 cups coconut milk

1/2 cup flax meal

2 tablespoons honey

1/4 teaspoon cloves

2 teaspoons cinnamon

1/4 teaspoon nutmeg

coconut flakes

sliced almonds

sunflower seeds

Place all the ingredients with the exception of the coconut flakes, sliced almonds and sunflower seeds into the slow cooker. Stir to combine.

On a high heat setting, you can heat up the ingredients for an hour. After one hour, turn the heat on low and let everything cook for another 5 hours.

When the porridge is done, serve in some bowls and garnish with the almonds, sunflower seeds, and coconut flakes.

Snacks/Appetizers

LAMB MEATBALLS

SNACKS&APPETIZERS › LAMB, EGGS, FENNEL, CAYENNE, TURMERIC, SAFFRON, ONION, GARLIC

2 pounds ground, grass-fed lamb

2 teaspoons cumin

2 teaspoons fennel

1 teaspoon cayenne

1/2 teaspoon turmeric

pinch of saffron

2 large organic eggs, lightly beaten

1/4 white onion, finely minced

3 cloves garlic, crushed

sea salt and freshly ground black pepper just before serving

1 tablespoon ghee

Heat the ghee in a frying pan over medium heat.

Mix all the ingredients in a bowl to combine well.

Shape into meatballs and drop into the pan.

Brown for 5 minutes, turning the meatballs once.

Add the meatballs into the slow cooker.

Add 1/4 cup chicken or beef stock, cover and cook on low for 3-4 hours.

SLOW COOKER ROASTED SPICY NUTS

SNACKS&APPETIZERS › PECANS, ALMONDS, PIS-
TACHIOS, PUMPKIN SEEDS, MAPLE SYRUP, CUR-
RY, ROSEMARY, CAYENNE, SALT

1 cup raw, unsalted pecans

1 cup raw, unsalted almonds

1 cup raw, unsalted pistachios (no shells)

1/2 cup raw, unsalted pumpkin seeds

1 1/2 tablespoons maple syrup

1 teaspoon curry

1 teaspoon rosemary

1/4 teaspoon cayenne pepper

1/2 teaspoon kosher salt

cooking spray

Use a 4 quart or bigger crockpot.

Spray the inside of the crockpot with cooking spray.

Put in the nuts, seeds, all of the spices and the maple syrup. Toss well to coat.

Cover and cook on high for 2 hours, stirring every 20 minutes. The nuts will burn if you don't stir.

Spread the nuts out on a layer of foil or wax paper to completely cool, and store in an air-tight container.

PALEO SPICY RIB

SNACKS&APPETIZERS PORK, PAPRIKA, CHILI, CAYENNE, BASIL, CUMIN

3 pounds pork spare ribs

2 tablespoons paprika

1 teaspoon chili powder

1 teaspoon cayenne

1 teaspoon sweet basil, dried

1 teaspoon cumin

sea salt and freshly ground black pepper to taste after dish is cooked

SAUCE

1 cup tomatoes, peeled and chopped

2 serrano peppers, chopped and peeled

2 tablespoons apple cider vinegar

3 cloves garlic, crushed

1/2 small onion, minced

1 tablespoon fresh lime juice

two pinches of sea salt

Cut ribs into single pieces.

Rub pieces with the spices and place in the slow cooker.

Put tomatoes in a bowl, smash them with a fork and mix in the rest of the sauce ingredients.

Pour mixture over the ribs, cover and cook on low for 4-6 hours until ribs are tender.

Add salt and pepper after cooking.

SLOW COOKER ITALIAN MEAT-BALLS IN MARINARA SAUCE

SNACKS&APPETIZERS › BEEF, ONION, EGGS, PARSLEY, TOMATO, OREGANO, BASIL

MEATBALLS

1 1/2 pounds, of grass-fed beef (or another meat of your choice)

1 large onion, diced small (set aside one half for the sauce)

4 cloves of minced garlic (set aside one half for the sauce)

1/3 cup almond flour

2 organic eggs, whisked

1/4 cup of fresh, chopped flat-leaf parsley

pinch of red pepper flakes

SAUCE

(1) 28 ounces can of San Marzano Plum Tomatoes in Sauce

(1) 15 ounces can of tomato sauce

the other half of the diced onions and minced garlic (see meat-ball ingredients above)

1 teaspoon of dried oregano

1 teaspoon of dried basil

2 tablespoons of fresh chopped parsley

1/2 to 1 teaspoon of sea salt

a pinch of red pepper flakes (optional)

Sauté onions in 2 tablespoons of olive oil for 5-7 minutes.

Season with salt, add garlic, and cook for one additional minute.

Remove from heat.

Add half of the onion/garlic to the slow cooker, and set the other half aside.

Add remaining ingredients for the sauce into the slow cooker.

Break apart the tomatoes in the slow cooker so they are not whole.

Set slow cooker to low.

Add ground beef to the bowl you set aside of the chopped onions and minced garlic.

Add the rest of the meatball ingredients to the same bowl.

Combine all the meatball ingredients with your hands – do not over mix or your meatballs will turn out tough.

Preheat a medium or large frying pan with few tablespoons of coconut or olive oil over medium heat.

Form meatballs by hand (about the size of a golf ball).

Place meatballs in the heated frying pan, to get a nice brown on the surface.

Transfer browned meatballs directly into the slow cooker

Cook in slow cooker on low 4-6 hours.

Garnish with fresh parsley and serve hot.

Enjoy!

PALEO SWEETY DRUMSTICKS

3 pounds chicken drumsticks

1/3 cup honey

2 tablespoons, stone ground mustard

3 cloves garlic, crushed

1/4 cup coconut oil

sea salt and pepper for browning and just before serving

Salt and pepper drumsticks and brown them in a broiler for 5 minutes, turning once.

Watch closely to make sure drumsticks don't burn.

Meanwhile, melt the coconut oil and mix it with the rest of the ingredients in a large bowl.

Place browned chicken in bowl and mix until coated with the sauce.

Pour everything into the slow cooker and cook on low for 5 hours.

Salt and pepper the drumsticks before serving.

PALEO STUFFED PEPPERS

SNACKS&APPETIZERS › BELL PEPPERS, CAULI-
FLOWER, TOMATO PASTE, HOT SAUSAGE, GAR-
LIC, BASIL, OREGANO, THYME

1 pound of ground Italian hot sausage

5 assorted bell peppers. (green, red, yellow)

1/2 head of cauliflower, grated or chopped into a "rice" consistency

1 small (8 ounce) can of tomato paste

1 small white onion, medium dice

1/2 head of garlic, minced

1 small handful of fresh basil, minced (or 2 teaspoons dried)

2 teaspoons dried oregano

2 teaspoons dried thyme

Cut the tops off of the peppers and scoop out and discard the seed (save the tops!)

Process or chop half a head of cauliflower into "rice" and put in a large mixing bowl.

Add the minced garlic, basil, dried herbs, and onion to your cauliflower and mix by hand.

Use a very hot skillet to lightly brown your sausage.

Add the sausage and can of tomato paste to your bowl of seasoned cauliflower and mix by hand.

Fit as much of the sausage mixture into your peppers as you can. Place the peppers into your slow cooker and loosely place the pepper tops back on.

Cook on low for 6 hours.

PALEO ASIAN CHICKEN WINGS

SNACKS&APPETIZERS › CHICKEN WINGS, GIN-GER, HOT SAUCE, HONEY, SESAME, GARLIC

1 tablespoon powdered ginger

1/2 cup coconut aminos

2 cloves of garlic, smashed

2 tablespoons of Sriracha hot sauce or Sambal Oelek chili paste

1 tablespoon of apple cider vinegar

1 tablespoon of raw honey

toasted sesame seeds and chopped green onions for garnish

3 to 4 pounds of chicken wings, browned

Brown the chicken wings.

Add all of the ingredients to a food processor or blender and pulse until an even consistency is reached.

Place the chicken in the slow cooker and cover with the sauce.

Cook on high for 2 hours or low for 4 hours.

Garnish with toasted sesame seeds and finely chopped green on-ions.

Soups/Stews

ROASTED PUMPKIN COCONUT SOUP

SOUPS&STEWS › PUMPKIN, GHEE, PEAR, CUMIN, CINNAMON, GINGER

1 small pie pumpkin

1 tablespoon of ghee or grass fed butter

2 medium carrots, peeled and chopped roughly

1 small Bartlett pear, peeled, cored, and chopped

4 cups of chicken stock

1 can of coconut milk

2 teaspoons cumin

2 teaspoons cinnamon

1 teaspoon ground ginger

1/2 teaspoon red pepper flakes (optional)

Preheat your oven to 350 degrees F.

Cut the top off of the pumpkin and then cut it in half. Large serrated knives can be easier. Then cut the pumpkin into quarters.

Coat the inner surfaces of the pumpkin sections with ghee or butter, partially melted works best.

Place the pumpkin shell side down in your baking pan with 1/2 cup water and bake for 20 to 25 minutes. You are looking for the pumpkin to pull away from the shell.

Allow the pumpkin to cool and then use a large fork to pull it from its shell, place it in a large bowl and mash it.

Add 4 cups of mashed pumpkin to the slow cooker, along with the rest of the ingredients.

Cook on low for 5 to 6 hours.

Use an immersion blender to puree the soup as desired, or transfer the contents of the slow cooker to a food processor or blender.

Optional: garnish with pumpkin seeds and enjoy!

CHICKEN AND KALE SOUP

SOUPS&STEWS › CHICKEN BREAST, SHALLOTS, GINGER, TOMATOES, CAYENNE, SQUASH, KALE

3 sliced shallots

1 tablespoon coconut oil

1 tablespoon ginger

8 ounces chicken breast

1 tablespoon garlic

1 can diced tomatoes

1/4 tablespoon cayenne pepper

2 squashes, chayote

4 cups broth

1/2 cup cashew butter

1 bunch of kale

pepper

Heat up the oil in a pot on the stove so it becomes hot. Add in the shallots and let them cook so they become crispy and brown.

Turn the heat down before adding in the cayenne, garlic, and ginger. Cook these ingredients another minute before adding in the chicken. Continue cooking.

Add in the broth before bringing everything to boil. Add in the kale, chayote, and tomatoes next before allowing everything to simmer so that the chicken can cook and the vegetables become tender.

Mix a little of the broth with the cashew butter before stirring it all back into the soup. Add these ingredients into the slow cooker and let it cook on low for 5 hours.

Season with the pepper and enjoy.

PALEO CHILI

SOUPS&STEWS › BEEF, ONION, BELL PEPPER, GARLIC, TOMATO, CHILI, MUSTARD, BASIL, CHILE PEPPER, CILANTRO

1 1/2 pounds ground beef

1 1/2 cups onion, chopped

1 cup green bell pepper, chopped

2 garlic cloves, minced

2 cans tomato sauce (15 ounces can each)

1 can diced tomato (14 ounces can)

2 - 3 teaspoons chili powder

1 - 2 teaspoons dry hot mustard

3/4 teaspoon dried basil

1/2 teaspoon black pepper

1 - 2 dried hot chili peppers

fresh cilantro leaves

cooked bacon crumbled for garnish (optional)

In a large skillet, cook and stir beef, onion, bell pepper, and garlic over medium-high heat (6 to 8 minutes). Drain fat. Transfer to slow cooker.

Add tomato sauce, diced tomatoes, chili powder, mustard basil, black pepper, and chili peppers (optional) into a slow cooker. Mix well. Cover and cook for 8 to 10 hours on low (4 to 5 hours on high).

Before serving, remove the chili.

FRENCH ONION SOUP

2 pounds sweet onions thinly sliced

3 cups beef broth

3 cups chicken broth

2 cups water

3 tablespoons coconut oil

1 1/2 teaspoon dried thyme

black pepper

Line bottom of the slow cooker with thinly sliced onions. Add 1 tablespoon coconut oil onto the onions.

Cover and cook for 10 – 12 hours on high to caramelize the onions. When caramelized, add in thyme, chicken and beef broths and water. Decrease crockpot settings to low and cook for 8 to 10 hours.

WHITE ACORN SQUASH SOUP

1 pound of ground turkey or chicken.

1 tablespoon of coconut oil, grass-fed butter, or ghee.

1 white acorn squash, peeled and diced into large or medium cubes.

4 cups of chicken stock.

4 to 6 cups of water.

1 medium red onion, diced.

2 cloves of garlic, minced.

2 teaspoons of dried parsley.

sea salt and black pepper to taste.

Add the cooking fat of choice to your pot/pan and set heat to medium.

Add the ground meat, garlic, parsley, salt, and pepper and stir.

Cook meat until browned yet not fully cooked, then add the squash.

Add 1 cup of the chicken stock to deglaze the pot/pat and stir well.

Transfer the contents of the pot/pan to the slow cooker.

Add the rest of the chicken stock and water to the slow cooker.

Cook on low for 4 to 6 hours.

PALEO BUTTERNUT SQUASH SOUP

SOUPS&STEWS › BUTTERNUT SQUASH, COCO-NUT MILK, APPLE, CARROT, CINNAMON, NUTMEG

1 large butternut squash (about 6 cups cubed)

1 can (14 ounces) coconut milk

2 cups of chicken stock

1 granny smith apple, peeled, cored, and cubed

2 carrots, peeled and chopped

1 teaspoon ground cinnamon

1 teaspoon ground nutmeg

Cook everything on low heat for 4 to 6 hours.

Blend or puree with an immersion blender when cooking is finished. If you don't have one, let your mix cool before transferring it to a blender or food processor.

Garnish with anything from cinnamon and nutmeg, to curry powder, pumpkin seeds, and bacon

OXTAIL SOUP

SOUPS&STEWS › SHITAKE MUSHROOMS, ONION, CHICKEN STOCK

3 pounds oxtails, cut into sections

1 onion, chopped

2 large carrots, sliced

1 large leek, cleaned well and sliced

2 bay leaves

1 red spicy pepper (optional)

3 cups beef stock

1 cup red wine

2 tomatoes, peeled and chopped

1 teaspoon thyme

1/4 cup chopped parsley, added at the end

sea salt and black pepper before serving

Brown the oxtail in a heavy-bottomed pan over medium-high heat in batches about 5 minutes each, then transfer to the slow cooker.

Put all ingredients in the slow cooker except the parsley.

Cook on low for 8 hours.

Stir in parsley, and add salt and pepper before serving

SLOW COOKER JAMBALAYA SOUP

SOUPS&STEWS › SHRIMP, SAUSAGE, CHICKEN, CAULIFLOWER, GARLIC, HOT SAUCE, SPICES

5 cups chicken stock.

4 peppers — any color, chopped

1 large onion, chopped

1 large can of organic diced tomatoes (leave the juice)

2 cloves garlic, diced

2 bay leafs

1 pound large shrimp, raw and de-veined.

4 ounces chicken, diced

1 package spicy Andouille sausage

1/2-1 head of cauliflower

2 cups okra (optional)

3 tablespoons Cajun Seasoning (see below the recipe for homemade)

1/4 cups hot sauce of your choice

Cajun Seasoning:

2 1/2 tablespoons paprika

2 tablespoons salt

2 tablespoons garlic powder

1 tablespoon black pepper

1 tablespoon onion powder

1 tablespoon cayenne pepper

1 tablespoon dried oregano

1 tablespoon dried thyme

Put the chopped peppers, onions, garlic, chicken, Cajun season-ing, red hot, and bay leafs in the crockpot with the chicken stock.

Set on low for 6 hours.

About 30 minutes before it is finished, toss in the cut up sausages.

While this is cooking quickly make cauliflower rice by pulsing raw cauliflower in the food processor until it resembles rice.

For the last 20 minutes, add in the cauliflower rice and the raw shrimp.

Enjoy!

MEAT LOVERS CHILI

SOUPS&STEWS › SAUSAGE, STEAK, SIRLOIN, ON-ION, BELL PEPPER, GARLIC, TOMATOES, CHILI, OREGANO, BAY LEAVES

6 ounces Italian sausage

1 pound round steak, chopped into even bite sized pieces

2 pounds ground sirloin

2 cups chopped yellow onion

1 1/2 cups bell pepper (combination of red and green)

8 cloves of garlic (minced)

2 (28 ounce) cans of chopped tomatoes with their juice

2 tablespoons chili powder

1 tablespoon Ancho chili pepper

1 tablespoon cumin

3 teaspoons tomato paste

1 teaspoon dried oregano

1/2 teaspoon fresh ground pepper and 1/2 teaspoon salt (adjust to your taste)

2 bay leaves

1/4 cup red wine (optional)

Heat a large pan over medium-high heat. Remove casings from sausage. Add all the meat, onion, bell pepper, and garlic to pan. Cook until meat is browned, stirring to crumble.

Add chili powder, Ancho chili pepper, cumin and tomato paste, oregano, salt, pepper and bay leaves. Cook 1 minute, stirring constantly. Stir in wine and tomatoes and bring to boil.

Transfer to slow cooker and let cook for 6 hours on low.

Discard bay leaves and serve.

SLOW COOKER BEEF STEW

SOUPS&STEWS › BEEF, ONION, BALSAMIC VIN-
EGAR, CELERY, CARROTS, POTATOES, GARLIC,
PAPRIKA, SPICES

2 pounds pastured stewing beef

2 cups of beef or chicken stock (or 1 cup stock and 1 cup wine or beer)

1 tablespoon balsamic vinegar

1 medium onion, chopped

2 stalks of celery, roughly chopped

2 large carrots, peeled and chopped

3-5 small potatoes, cubed (optional)

1 to 3 cloves of garlic, minced (to taste)

1 tablespoon of paprika

3 bay leaves

1/2 teaspoon of salt

1/2 teaspoon of black pepper

1 teaspoon each dried rosemary, basil, and oregano

1/8 cup arrowroot powder (if you want to thicken your stew)

Place meat into slow cooker.

Add liquids then all other ingredients except for arrowroot powder on top.

Cover and cook on low for 8 hours.

Directions to thicken:

Just before you're ready to eat, use a ladle to spoon out most of the liquid into a small saucepan.

Bring to a boil.

Stir a small amount of the liquid into a small bowl and sprinkle in the arrowroot flour, whisking as you add it. Make sure there are no lumps.

Slowly pour the arrowroot mixture into the boiling liquid in the pot and remove from heat as you whisk continuously.

Do not reheat as this will break the bonds of the thickener.

If it's not thick enough, use water and some more arrowroot powder in your small bowl, whisk to mix, then slowly add into the gravy.

Pour thickened gravy back into slow cooker and stir gently.

PALEO CROCKPOT BORSCHT

1 pound beef stew meat

3 - 4 large beets, peeled and chopped into large pieces

2 white potatoes, peeled and chopped into large pieces

1 onion, minced

2 carrots, chopped into bite-sized pieces

1 28 ounces can diced tomatoes

2 cups beef broth

4 cloves garlic, minced

1 6 ounce can tomato paste

6 tablespoons red wine vinegar

3 tablespoons maple syrup

1 1/2 teaspoon dill

1 teaspoon parsley

1 teaspoon salt

1 teaspoon black pepper

1 bay leaf

1 small - medium head of cabbage, shredded

Brown beef stew meat in a large pan.

Sauté the onions.

Plop beef stew meat, beets, potatoes, diced tomatoes, carrots and onion in the slow cooker.

In a large bowl, mix together beef broth, garlic, tomato paste, red wine vinegar, maple syrup, dill, parsley, salt and pepper. Pour mixture over the rest in the slow cooker.

Cook on low for 8-9 hours.

Turn slow cooker to high and add cabbage, mixing it well into the borscht. Cook for another 30 minutes.

Serve with optional garnishes of sour cream or yogurt.

PALEO SLOW COOKER BEEF AND MUSHROOM STEW

SOUPS&STEWS › BEEF, MUSHROOMS, SWEET POTATO, GARLIC, ONION, BALSAMIC VINEGAR, ROSEMARY, SAGE, PARSLEY

1.5-2 pounds beef stew meat

1 package sliced button mushrooms

1 package whole shiitake mushrooms

1 package baby Portobello mushrooms

1 sweet potato, chopped

4 garlic cloves, peeled and smashed (use the flat part of a knife)

1 cup pearl onions, placed in warm water for 5 minutes then peeled

1 cup chicken or beef broth (or water)

1/3 cup balsamic vinegar

2 tablespoons red wine vinegar

1 bay leaf

2 tablespoons onion powder

1 tablespoon dried rosemary

1 teaspoon dried sage

1 teaspoon dried parsley

sea salt and freshly ground black pepper, to taste

Place all mushrooms, garlic, and pearl onions in the bottom of the slow cooker.

Put meat and sweet potatoes on top.

Add the rest of the ingredients (put all the spices on top of the meat and sweet potatoes).

Cook on low for 6-8 hours.

Serve.

PALEO GREEK STEW

SOUPS&STEWS › BEEF, GARLIC, ONION, BAY LEAVES, RED WINE, CINNAMON, TOMATO, CLOVES, WALNUT

3 pounds ground beef

3 tablespoons coconut oil

10 garlic cloves

1 chopped onion

2 bay leaves

1/2 cup red wine, dry

2 tablespoons red wine vinegar

1 cup tomato puree

1 cinnamon stick

fresh black pepper

4 cloves

2 tablespoons currants

1 pound pearl onions

1 cup walnut halves

In a pan, heat up coconut oil before placing the meat inside and letting it brown for around 5 minutes. Take the meat out of the pan and place into a bowl.

Add the garlic cloves and onion to the pan and cook for 4 minutes so the onions can become translucent. Add in the wine vinegar, wine, and tomato puree before adding the meat back in as well.

Add the cloves, cinnamon, and bay leaves along with some pepper to season.

Place everything inside a slow cooker and let cook for about 1 hour on high.

Add in the currants and pearl onions and cook until the meat is falling off the bone.

Serve with walnuts and enjoy.

PORK LOIN AND BUTTERNUT SQUASH STEW

2 1/2 pounds pork loin cubed

2 leeks, trimmed and sliced

2 shallots diced

4 celery stalks, chopped

4 cups butternut squash, cubed

7 - 10 garlic cloves, thinly sliced

2 teaspoons garam masala

1 1/2 teaspoons lemon juice

1 cup chicken broth

1/4 cup coconut milk

Place pork loin and vegetables (leeks, shallots, celery, butternut squash, and cloves) into the slow cooker. Sprinkle masala over the pork and vegetables.

Pour the broth, lemon juice and coconut milk into the slow cooker. With a large spoon, mix all ingredients.

Cook for 7 hours on low.

Serve hot.

SAGE STEW WITH CHERRIES AND PUMPKIN

4 cups butternut squash

2 pounds stew meat

1 chopped onion

1 cup dried cherries

1 teaspoon thyme

1 tablespoon sage

1 bay leaf

1 teaspoon allspice

3 1/2 cup beef stock

1/2 teaspoon nutmeg

1 cup pumpkin pureed

1 tablespoon butter (grass fed)

In a saucepan melt the butter. When the butter is melted, add in the thyme, sage, and onions until they are soft.

In a skillet, sear the meat so that a crust begins to form. Add the onion mixture and the meat to the slow cooker along with the allspice, bay leaf, nutmeg, and beef stock. Set the slow cooker on low and let it cook for about 6 hours.

After 6 hours, add in the cherries and the butternut squash and let it all cook for another 2 hours.

Right before it is time to serve, add in the pumpkin puree and season with pepper before enjoying!

Meat Dishes

SLOW COOKER PUERCO PIBIL

MEAT DISHES › PORK SHOULDER, TOMATO, ON-ION, CUMIN, NUTMEG, ORANGE, SPICES

1 medium onion

15 ounce can of diced fire-roasted tomato

2 tablespoon annatto powder (or paprika)

1 teaspoon ground cumin

1 teaspoon ground black pepper

1 teaspoon sea salt

pinch of nutmeg

5 pounds pork shoulder roast

1 orange, juiced

1/4 cup apple cider vinegar

2 teaspoons salt

In a small bowl, mix the annatto, cumin, black pepper, 1 teaspoon salt and pinch of nutmeg. Stir in a bit of water until the spices have a thick, paste-like consistency.

Slice the onion and add to a skillet with a spoonful of fat (coconut oil, olive oil) over medium heat. Cook for a few minutes until translucent, then add the can of tomatoes. Cook for a few more minutes until softened.

Prepare the pork by trimming off any large pieces of external fat (the fat on the inside of the meat will cook out). Slice each roast into long pieces about 1.5 inches wide. Season with salt.

In the slow cooker, mix the juice of one orange with the cider vinegar. Add the annatto / spice paste and stir until dissolved. Lay the pork into the liquid. Top with the tomato / onion mixture.

Cook on low for 6-8 hours.

Skim the excess fat off the top while it's still warm.

Enjoy!

PALEO TEXMEX CARNITAS

MEAT DISHES › PORK, ONION, GREEN CHILES, CUMIN, HONEY, LIME& ORANGE JUICE, SPICES

2-3 pounds pork (butt or shoulder for best results)

1/4 cup diced yellow onions

1/4 cup diced green chilies (canned is okay)

1 teaspoon fresh minced garlic

1 1/4 cup (1 small can) diced tomatoes

1 tablespoon cumin

2 teaspoons onion powder

2 teaspoons chili powder

1 teaspoons garlic powder

1/2 teaspoon salt

1 tablespoon agave/honey

2 teaspoons lime juice

2 tablespoons orange juice

1/2 cup barbecue sauce

Place all ingredients in a slow cooker on low 6-8 hours.

About an hour prior to eating, shred the pork with a fork and stir.

Serve in lettuce bowls/wraps.

SLOW COOKER APPLE PORK TENDERLOIN

MEAT DISHES › PORK TENDERLOIN, APPLES, NUTMEG, HONEY

4 organic Gala apples

1 1/2 pound — 2 pounds pork tenderloin

nutmeg

2 tablespoons raw honey (optional)

Core and slice the apples.

Add a layer of apples in the bottom of the slow cooker and sprinkle with nutmeg.

Place slits in the pork tenderloin and cut tenderloin in half if you need to so it can lay nice in the crockpot.

Take one apple slice and place in each slit in the tenderloin.

Place tenderloin with apple slices in place into the slow cooker on top of the layer of apples and sprinkle top with nutmeg.

Place remaining apple slices on top of the pork tenderloin and sprinkle once more with nutmeg.

Place slow cooker on low for 8-9 hours.

Enjoy!

PALEO BALSAMIC ROAST

MEAT DISHES › BEEF, SWEET POTATOES, CARROT

3 pounds beef chuck roast, boneless

2 to 3 sweet potatoes, cut into big pieces

4 carrots, cut into big pieces and 1 onion, sliced

2 sprigs of fresh rosemary and 2 bay leaves

2 cloves garlic, minced

1 cup red wine (optional)

1/3 cup balsamic vinegar

1 1/2 cup beef stock and 2 tablespoons cooking fat

sea salt and freshly ground black pepper to taste

Season the roast on all sides with sea salt and black pepper. Melt the cooking fat over a medium-high heat in a large skillet, and sear the roast for 2-3 minutes on each side.

Place the meat in the slow cooker and top with the onion, minced garlic, balsamic vinegar, beef stock, bay leaves and red wine (optional). Cover the slow cooker and cook on low for 6 hours.

Add the carrots and sweet potatoes, set the slow cooker to high, and cook for another 3-4 hours, or until the vegetables are nice and soft. Remove the 2 bay leaves. Pour the liquid from the slow cooker into a saucepan and bring to a slow boil over a medium-high heat. Keep it boiling and let it reduce until you get the desired consistency for the sauce. Pour the sauce back and serve with the meat and vegetables.

VERY SIMPLE HAWAIIAN PULLED PORK

MEAT DISHES › PORK SHOULDER, PINEAPPLE, GINGER

3-4 pounds pork shoulder

1 can crushed or cubed pineapple (in water)

2 tablespoons grated ginger (or 1/2 teaspoons dry)

Put pork in the slow cooker.

Dump the pineapple on top with all the liquid, too.

Add the ginger.

Cook on low for 6-8 hours.

SLOW COOKED SALMON

MEAT DISHES › SALMON, GARLIC, LEMON, SHALLOT, ROSEMARY, THYME

2 pounds salmon fillets, cut across the fish into 4 pieces

2 cloves garlic, crushed

1/2 cup white wine

2 tablespoons fresh lemon juice

1 teaspoon lemon zest

4 shallots, sliced

2 tablespoons macadamia-nut oil

1/2 teaspoon rosemary

1/2 teaspoon thyme

sea salt and ground black pepper just before serving

Place salmon in the slow cooker skin side down.

Add the garlic, white wine, lemon juice and zest to the slow cooker, making sure the garlic is in the liquid.

Place the sliced shallots on top of the fillets and drizzle the oil over the fish.

Sprinkle the dried herbs over the fillets and sauce, then cook on low for 1 1/2 to 2 hours.

Reduce remaining liquid on the stovetop by half over medium-low heat for about 5 minutes, and pour over the plated salmon.

Salt and pepper to taste. Serve.

PALEO BEEF BOURGUIGNON

MEAT DISHES › BEEF, BACON, GARLIC, SHAL-
LOTS, CARROTS, MUSHROOMS, RED WINE, CO-
GNAC

1/2 pound quality, uncured bacon, diced

2 pounds grass-fed beef chuck, big cubed

8 shallots, peeled and left whole

2 cloves garlic, crushed

1 tablespoon Herbes de Provence

1 pound mushrooms, stems removed and sliced

1 pound carrots, sliced

1 1/2 cups red wine

1 cup beef stock

1/2 cup cognac

sea salt and pepper just before serving

Sauté the bacon over medium high until just crisp, about 3-5 minutes.

Remove the bacon and brown the meat in the bacon grease in batches for about 5 minutes each, turning the meat only a few times and allowing it to brown well.

If the bacon grease is smoking, turn the heat down to medium.

Place the beef, bacon and all other ingredients into the slow cooker and cook on low for 6-8 hours.

You may have extra liquid, so use a slotted spoon to serve the meat and vegetables in a bowl and then ladle just enough sauce over the dish to cover the bottom of the bowl.

Salt and pepper before serving.

LEMON GARLIC CHICKEN

MEAT DISHES › CHICKEN, LEMON, ONION, GAR-
LIC, ITALIAN SEASONING

1 whole organic chicken

1 whole lemon

1 white onion, sliced

30-40 garlic cloves, peeled

freshly ground black pepper, to taste

Italian seasoning (for homemade use marjoram, thyme, savory, sage, rosemary, basil, and oregano, equal amounts of each)

Wash whole chicken under running cold water. Pat dry with paper towel.

Squeeze lemon juice all over the chicken. Place the lemon halves into the chicken's cavity. Then season chicken with generous amounts of salt, pepper, and Italian seasoning.

Place sliced onions and peeled garlic at bottom of the slow cooker. Spread evenly.

Place chicken into the crockpot on top of the onions and garlic. Close the lid and cook on low for 6 hours.

When complete, remove chicken and place on cutting board. Shred the chicken and return into the slow cooker. Discard the carcass. Mix until chicken is well incorporated into the broth.

BEEF BRISKET

MEAT DISHES › BEEF BRISKET, SHALLOTS, PARS-
NIPS, TOMATOES, BAY LEAVES, CHILI

3-4 pounds grass-fed beef brisket

3-4 shallots, peeled

2 parsnips, chopped (you can substitute 2 carrots)

2 tomatoes, chopped and peeled

2 bay leaves

1 cup beef broth

2 tablespoons apple-cider vinegar

2 tablespoons chili powder

1 teaspoon dry mustard

sea salt and freshly ground black pepper just before serving

Preheat a heavy-bottomed pan to medium high for a couple minutes and brown the brisket all sides for about 6-8 minutes.

Transfer the meat to the slow cooker.

Add the rest of the ingredients to the slow cooker, making sure the dried spices are mixed into the liquid and not clumped or sitting dry on top of the meat.

Cook on low for 6-8 hours.

Add salt and pepper, slice against the grain and serve in slices, spooning the sauce over the meat.

SLOW COOKER TACOS

MEAT DISHES · PORK, ONION, CHILI, PINEAPPLE, GARLIC, SPICES

(1) 3 pound pork shoulder, roast, or tenderloin.

6 dried guajillo chili peppers (rehydrated in water) or 6 chipotles in adobo sauce

(1) 8 ounce can crushed pineapple, or 2 cups of fresh pineapple, chopped.

1 cup of white onion, diced.

1/2 cup of orange juice, or the juice of two large oranges.

4 cloves of garlic, smashed.

1 tablespoon of apple cider vinegar.

1 teaspoon of oregano.

1 teaspoon of cinnamon.

1 teaspoon of cumin.

1 teaspoon of black pepper.

1 teaspoon of sea salt.

one large ziploc bag for the pork to marinade in.

salsa garnish: equal amounts of pineapple, white onion, and cilantro with a touch of lime juice.

If using dried chilies, boil them in a small saucepan until fully rehydrated and softened, then drain.

In a blender or food processor, combine the chilies, pineapple, orange juice, garlic, onion, vinegar, and spices.

Puree the marinade until an even consistency is obtained.

Trim all excess fat off of the cut of pork.

Place the pork in the large ziploc bag and pour in the marinade.

Make sure the pork is evenly coated and remove as much air as possible from the bag before sealing.

Let the pork marinade for at least 2 hours.

Dump the pork and marinade into the slow cooker.

Cook on low for 6 to 8 hours.

Shred or slice the pork as you see fit, mixing in some of the marinade and pork juices.

Serve in crisp lettuce wraps.

Garnish with a simple salsa made of equal parts pineapple, white onion, and cilantro, with a touch of lime juice.

Enjoy!

STUFFED EGGPLANT

MEAT DISHES › EGGPLANT, BEEF, BASIL, MINT, CUMIN, CAYENNE, GARLIC, GHEE, ONION, TOMATOES

6 eggplants

1 pound ground beef

1 tablespoon fresh basil, chopped

2 tablespoons fresh mint, chopped

1 teaspoon cumin

1/8 teaspoon cayenne

2 garlic cloves, minced

2 tablespoons ghee

1/2 red onion, minced

2 Anaheim peppers, diced

3 tomatoes, chopped and peeled

sea salt and freshly ground black pepper to taste

more salt and pepper just before serving

Cut eggplants lengthwise and scoop out the inside and reserve, leaving the shell about a half an inch thick.

Cube the inside of the eggplant meat.

Add to the ground beef the basil, mint, cumin, cayenne, salt, pepper and garlic.

Heat the ghee in a heavy-bottomed pan over medium high and sauté the onions, peppers, and approximately one-third of the tomato and all the scooped-out eggplant for 5 minutes until the onions are translucent.

Add the ground beef and brown for 5 minutes, breaking up the meat with a wooden spoon or spatula.

Scoop the mixture into the eggplant shells and place them in the slow cooker.

Arrange the rest of the tomatoes around the eggplant.

Cook on low for 3-4 hours.

Salt and pepper to taste, then serve.

MOROCCAN CHICKEN

MEAT DISHES › CHICKEN THIGHS, TOMATO SAUCE, GINGER, LEMON, ONION, GARLIC, PAPRIKA

1 (14 oz.) tomato sauce

1/3 cup apricot puree or jam

juice of small lemon

1 teaspoon ground ginger

1 teaspoon cumin

1 teaspoon sea salt

1/2 teaspoon sweet paprika

4 pounds chicken thighs

2 yellow onions, sliced

1 tablespoon ginger, grated

3 garlic cloves, minced

3 cinnamon sticks

3 tablespoons coconut oil

1/2 cup almond butter

1–2 cups water

In a bowl, combine then mix tomato sauce, apricot, cumin, ground ginger, lemon juice, paprika, and salt. Over medium-high heat, warm frying pan and add 2 tablespoons of coconut oil.

Pat dry the chicken thighs and place into the heated oil. Brown all sides for 3 to 4 minutes per side. Transfer the browned chicken into the crockpot.

Add onions, ginger and garlic to the pan and cook for 2 minutes. When translucent, transfer into crockpot.

Turn off the heat. Pour the tomato-apricot mixture into the pan. Deglaze. Take a spoon to scrape the browned bits. Mix in 1 cup of water and the almond butter into the mixture. Stir. Pour mixture over the chicken in the crockpot. Toss in cinnamon sticks. Add more water, just enough to cover the meat partially.

Cover and cook for 6 hours on low.

ROTISSERIE CHICKEN

MEAT DISHES › CHICKEN, SWEET POTATOES

1 whole chicken

sea salt and freshly ground pepper

4-5 small sweet potatoes

extra virgin olive oil

Rub sweet potatoes with oil and sprinkle with salt and pepper. Wrap each potato in aluminum foil and place in crockpot.

Sprinkle chicken with a generous amount of salt and pepper. Place chicken on top of wrapped potatoes. Cover and cook for 4 – 6 hours on low.

Remove chicken. Be careful as meat will fall off the bone (this is okay). Carefully remove potatoes, unwrap. Serve chicken and potatoes together.

ROSEMARY LEMON GARLIC LAMB AND SWEET POTATO NOODLES

MEAT DISHES › LEG OF LAMB, GARLIC, ROSE-MARY, SWEET POTATOES

1/2 leg of lamb

3–4 rosemary stalks

3–4 garlic cloves, peeled

juice and zest of lemon

1/2 cup chicken stock

2 sweet potatoes

1–2 tablespoons coconut oil

2 tablespoons olive oil

freshly ground black pepper

flat leaf parsley

Wash leg of lamb and pat dry. Season with pepper.

In a food processor, throw in rosemary leaves, lemon zest and garlic cloves. Process until well mixed. Add olive oil and mix again.

Spread paste all over lamb. Refrigerate lamb for one hour, or overnight.

After one hour, or next day, place lamb in slow cooker. Pour 1/2 cup chicken stock and lemon juice over the lamb. Cook on low heat for 6-8 hours.

When ready, remove lamb and place on chopping board. Rest it for 10 minutes.

For the Sweet Potatoes: Peel potatoes cutting each into thirds. Using a spiral cutter, cut potatoes into long strands (or manually cut potatoes into long thin strands).

In a skillet, heat coconut oil over medium-heat. When oil is hot, add in potato noodles and season with salt and pepper according to taste.

Place noodles with slices of lamb on a plate and serve.

PEPPER VENISON ROAST

MEAT DISHES › VENISON ROAST, ONION, CAR-
ROTS, CELERY, GARLIC, BLACK PEPPERCORNS,
OREGANO, BASIL

2-3 pounds venison roast

3 tablespoons butter

2 onions, chopped

2 carrots, chopped

2 stalks celery, diced

3 cloves garlic, crushed

1 1/2 tablespoons black peppercorns

1 cup beef broth

1 tablespoon parsley

1/2 teaspoon oregano

1/2 teaspoon basil

sea salt just before serving

Heat a heavy-bottomed pan over medium high heat. Add 1 tablespoon of the butter and brown the roast on all sides, about 8
minutes total.

Add meat to the slow cooker.

Lower heat on the stove to medium and melt the remaining butter.

Crack the peppercorns with a mortar and pestle or by rolling over the corns with a wine bottle.

Sauté the onions, carrots, celery and about one-third of the pepper until the onions are translucent, about 5 minutes.

Add the garlic and sauté another 3 minutes until fragrant.

Place mixture in slow cooker around the roast.

Add the beef broth.

Sprinkle in the oregano and basil getting some on the roast and some in the sauce.

Spread the remaining black pepper on the top of the roast.

Cook on low for 6-8 hours.

Salt to taste. Let rest for at least 10 minutes before carving and serving.

LAMB WITH POMEGRANATE SAUCE

MEAT DISHES › LAMB CHOPS, SHALLOTS, ONION, GARLIC, POMEGRANATE JUICE, WINE, HONEY, THYME, TARRAGON

3-4 pounds lamb chops

2 tablespoons ghee

4 shallots

1 onion

2 cloves garlic, crushed

1 cup pomegranate juice

1/2 cup red wine

1 tablespoon honey

1 teaspoon thyme

1 teaspoon tarragon

sea salt and black pepper just before serving

Melt ghee in a heavy-bottomed pan over medium heat.

Sauté the shallots and onions until translucent, about 5 minutes.

Add the garlic and cook another 3 minutes until fragrant.

Add the wine, pomegranate juice and honey and reduce for 5 minutes on medium low.

Add the lamb to the slow cooker, pour the wine mixture over it and sprinkle with the thyme and tarragon.

Cook on low for 6-8 hours.

Salt and pepper to taste, then serve.

Crack the peppercorns with a mortar and pestle or by rolling over.

SALSA PORK CHOPS

MEAT DISHES › PORK CHOPS, GARLIC, CUMIN, SALSA, LIME

4 pork chops, trim fat

1/2 teaspoons garlic powder

1/2 teaspoons ground cumin

1/2 teaspoons pepper

1 tablespoon olive oil

1 cup salsa, mild

2 tablespoons lime juice, freshly squeezed

Trim fat around pork.

In a small bowl, combine cumin, and pepper then rub the mixture into all sides of the pork chop.

In a heavy frying pan, heat oil over medium heat. Fry pork chops until well-browned, five minutes per side.

With olive oil, grease all sides of the slow cooker and place the browned pork chops in. Pour the salsa mixture, and lime into the crockpot. Set crockpot on high for two to three hours.

RED CURRY PORK MEDALLIONS

MEAT DISHES › PORK TENDERLOIN, RED CURRY, ONION

2 pound pork tenderloin, sliced into 1/2 inch thick medallion rounds.

2 tablespoons of red curry paste.

1/2 can of coconut milk.

1 white or yellow onion, sliced.

Pour the coconut milk into the slow cooker and stir the curry paste in well.

Drop the pork into the coconut curry mixture and make sure all pieces are evenly coated, and then about as flat as possible.

Layer the sliced onions evenly along the top of the pork.

Cook on low for 4 to 6 hours.

Vegeterian Dishes

BUTTERNUT SQUASH AND CA-SHEW CURRY

VEGETARIAN DISHES › BUTTERNUT SQUASH, ON-ION, CASHEWS, CURRY, CUMIN, GINGER, CHILI

1 medium to large butternut squash, cubed

1 medium red onion, chopped into smaller chunks

1 cup whole raw cashews

1 can (14.5 ounces) coconut milk

1 tablespoon curry powder

1/2 teaspoon cumin

1/2 teaspoon red chili paste

1 tablespoon ginger, freshly grated

3 garlic cloves, finely minced

juice of one lime

pinch of black pepper

Peel and cube the butternut squash.

Make the curry sauce first: put the coconut milk in the crockpot and add the garlic, ginger, lime and spices. Mix well.

Add the chopped onion to the mix and then dump the butternut squash over the top. You'll want to sort of mix the butternut squash in with the curry sauce, but don't worry about getting it totally sauced up.

Let the veggies steam away on low for 5-6 hours.

BACKED SWEET POTATOES

VEGETARIAN DISHES › SWEET POTATOES

2 large sweet potatoes

Wash off the sweet potatoes.

Don't dry them. You want the moisture in the crock.

Stab each sweet potato with a fork 5-6 times.

Plop them in the crockpot. Cover it.

Cook on low for 5-6 hours.

Enjoy!

SPAGHETTI ALLA CARBONARA

2 medium zucchinis (using spiral slicer, slice to create long thin-noodle like strings)

1/4 to 1/2 pounds pancetta, diced

4 eggs at room temperature

1/4 cup coconut milk

3 garlic cloves

minced black pepper to taste

Italian flat leaf parsley

Optional: grated parmesan

In a bowl, whisk eggs and coconut milk. Add a pinch of black pepper. Heat large pot over medium to high heat. Throw in the pancetta and cook until gold and crispy (five minutes). When cooked, remove and place into a bowl. Lower heat to medium.

Throw in the minced garlic into the pot until aromatic. Add zucchini noodles. Stir noodles and cook until tender and water evaporates (five minutes).

Throw this mixture along with the pancetta mixture and egg mixture into the slow cooker. Stirring quickly, coat the noodles with the mixture. Cook on a low setting for 4-5 hours, making sure not to overcook the eggs.

Garnish dish with pancetta, parsley and grated parmesan.

FALL SPICED ACORN SQUASH

VEGETARIAN DISHES › ACORN SQUASH, APPLE-
SAUCE, WALNUTS, DRIED CRANBERRIES, CINNA-
MON, NUTMEG

acorn squash, cut in half

4 heaping tablespoons applesauce

2 1/2 tablespoons chopped walnuts (or pecans)

2 1/2 tablespoons dried cranberries

1/8 teaspoon cinnamon

dash nutmeg

Carefully chop the acorn squash. Plop it in the slow cooker, fleshy parts facing up.

Mix the rest of the ingredients together and spoon them over the squash pieces in the slow cooker.

Pour just a bit of water around the squash (no more than a cup) so the acorn squash doesn't dry out during cooking.

Cook on low for 4 hours. The squash should be easily pierced with a fork when done.

SLOW COOKER RATATOUILLE

VEGETARIAN DISHES › EGGPLANT, ZUCCHINI, GARLIC, PARSLEY, SPICES

2 large onions, cut in half and sliced

1 large eggplant, sliced, cut in 2 inch pieces

4 small zucchini, sliced

2 garlic cloves, minced

2 large green bell peppers, de-seeded and cut into thin strips

2 large tomatoes, cut into 1/2 inch wedges

1 (6 ounce) can tomato paste

1 teaspoon dried basil

1/2 teaspoon oregano

1 teaspoon raw honey

2 teaspoons sea salt

1/2 teaspoon freshly ground black pepper

2 tablespoons fresh parsley, chopped

1/4 cup olive oil

red pepper flakes, to spice it up

Layer half the vegetables in a large crock pot in the following order: onion, eggplant, zucchini, garlic, green peppers and tomatoes.

Next sprinkle half the basil, oregano, sugar, parsley, salt and pepper on the veggies.

Dot with half of the tomato paste.

Repeat layering process with remaining vegetables, spices and tomato paste.

Drizzle with olive oil.

Cover and cook on low for 7 to 9 hours.

Refrigerate to store.

Desserts

PALEO PUMPKIN BUTTER

DESERTS › PUMPKIN, APPLE CIDER, HONEY, MAPLE SYRUP

1 can (15 ounces) pure pumpkin (or 15 ounces fresh pumpkin puree)

1/3 cup apple cider

1/4 cup honey

1/4 cup maple syrup

1 heaping tsp. pumpkin pie spice

Mix everything together well in the slow cooker.

Cook on low for 4 hours. It will still be liquidly and runny when it's technically done, but it firms up when you cool it down in the fridge.

Store it in the refrigerator and enjoy with apples, on cold chicken leftovers, on top of cooked squash or just straight on a spoon!

SPICED PEARS WITH STRAWBER-RY COULIS

DESSERTS › PEARS, LEMON, RAISINS, ALMONDS, CLOVES, NUTMEG, CINNAMON, HONEY

8 green pears, peeled and cored

1 lemon, juicy

1/4 orange rind

1/2 cup raisins

1/2 cup silvered almonds

8 cloves

1/2 teaspoons nutmeg

1/4 teaspoons cinnamon

1 1/2 cups white wine

2 tablespoons raw honey

2 teaspoons coconut sugar

250 grams strawberries

Place peeled and cored pears stalk up in the slow cooker. Stick a clove into each pear, close to the stalk. Drizzle lemon juice over each pear. Sprinkle almonds and raisins over the pears. Pour wine into the slow cooker. Drop the orange rind and honey into the wine.

Cook for five hours - 2 hours on low, then 3 hours on high.

Strawberry Coulis: Cut strawberries into quarters. In a pan add strawberries, coconut sugar and 1 tablespoon water. Cover with lid and bring to a boil. Once it starts to boil, turn down the heat and simmer for fifteen minutes (or until strawberries are soft). Puree the strawberry mixture and pour over pears. Serve with coconut cream.

PALEO BANANA COCONUT FOSTER

10 bananas, cut into quarters

1/2 cup chopped walnuts

1 cup coconut flakes

1 teaspoon ground cinnamon

1/4 cup honey

1/2 cup coconut oil, melted

2 teaspoons lemon zest

1/4 cup lemon juice

1 tablespoon coconut rum

1 teaspoons vanilla

coconut cream for serving

Place the bananas in the slow cooker and top with walnuts and coconut flakes.

Mix together remaining ingredients, except the coconut cream, and pour over the bananas.

Cook on low for 1 1/2-2 hours, or until bananas are tender, but not mushy.

Place on plates, pour coconut cream over and serve.

HONEY POACHED PEARS

DESERTS › HONEY, PEARS, GINGER, ORANGE JUICE

4 pears

2/3 cup honey

1 tablespoon water

pinch nutmeg

generous pinch ground ginger

1 tablespoon arrowroot powder

2 tablespoon orange juice

Core your pears from the bottom, leaving the top stems attached. Put them upright in the crockpot.

Mix the honey, water and ginger together and pour over the pears.

Cook on high for 2-3 hours. The pears should be tender and easily pierced with a fork, but not mushy.

Remove the pears from the crockpot; set aside. Add the arrowroot powder and orange juice to the juices left on the bottom of the slower cooker and mix well. Continue to cook on high for another ten or fifteen minutes until the sauce is thick(er).

Spoon over the pears and serve.

CROCKPOT APPLESAUCE

DESSERTS › APPLE, PEARS, CINNAMON, ORANGE
JUICE, VANILLA, HONEY

6 apples, peeled, cored and cut into thin slices

2 pears, peeled, cored and cut into thin slices

1 teaspoon cinnamon

1 teaspoon vanilla extract

2 tablespoons honey

juice from 1/2 tangelo or orange

1/2 teaspoon cloves

1/2 teaspoon nutmeg

Combine all ingredients in slow cooker.

Cook on low for 6 hours stirring occasionally if possible.

Use an immersion blender or food processor to puree the sauce.

STUFFED APPLES

DESSERTS › APPLE, COCONUT CREAM, ALMOND
BUTTER, CINNAMON, NUTMEG

4 green apples, cored (not all the way through, keep bottom intact)

1/2 cup coconut cream, or coconut butter, melted

1/4 cup almond butter

2 tablespoons cinnamon

1 pinch nutmeg

1 pinch sea salt

3 – 4 tablespoons unsweetened shredded coconut

1 cup water

Set aside cored apples with their bottoms still intact. Mix together coconut butter, almond butter, cinnamon, salt and nutmeg.

Place cored apples into the slow cooker. Pour water into the slow cooker. Spoon the butter mixture into each apple. Fill to the top of the apple.

Top each apple with more cinnamon and shredded coconut. Set crockpot on low and cook for 2 to 3 hours.

BERRY CRUMBLE

DESKtops

DESSERTS › BERRIES, COCONUT OIL, ALMOND MEAL

5 – 6 cups berries (strawberries, blackberries, blueberries)

3 tablespoons coconut oil, melted

1 cup almond meal

In large mixing bowl, add berries and 1 tablespoon coconut oil. Mix, then place into a slow cooker.

In the same mixing bowl, put 1 cup almond meal and 2 tablespoons melted coconut oil. Mix until it creates a crumbly mixture.

Sprinkle the almond crumble over the fruit. Cover and cook for 2 hours on low. Serve and enjoy.

PUMPKIN SPICED LATTES

DESSERTS › COCONUT MILK, PUMPKIN, AGAVE, VANILLA, CINNAMON, GINGER

1 can (14 ounces) coconut milk

1 cup strong brewed coffee

3 tablespoons canned pumpkin

1 tablespoons agave nectar

2 tablespoons vanilla extract

1/4 teaspoons cinnamon

1/8 teaspoons cloves

1/8 teaspoons nutmeg

dash of ginger

Mix everything together in the crockpot.

Cook on low for 2-3 hours.

Drizzle in a bit of honey if you want your latte to be sweeter.

WHAT THE PALEO DIET LOOKS LIKE?

To make it easy and understandable, Paleo is about eating the same whole foods that were found in nature several hundred thousand years ago. Whole foods have high levels of protein and fat, are low in carbohydrates and are free of ingredients we can't pronounce. The best examples are meats, vegetables, fruits, nuts, and seeds.

We want to replicate the benefits of the pre-agricultural diet without replicating the Stone Age methods. We aim to eat foods that were commonly available to our hunter-gatherer ancestors, not processed and packaged in a factory. Luckily, we can obtain the same Paleolithic results with foods available in grocery stores and farmers' markets.

What to avoid?

To be strong and healthy it's important not only what you eat, but also what you don't eat. Adding healthy ingredients in your diet is only half the Paleo plan. The other half implicates to exclude foods that will cause you problems (slow your metabolism and digestion, cause blood sugar problems and encourage fat storage). You should exclude refined sugars, alcohol, processed foods, grains and legumes

Refined sugars

It's best to avoid all sugars. White sugar, HFCS (high fructose corn syrup), chocolate, candy, soda and even artificial sweeteners are all "off limits". You can use raw honey in moderation as an occasional treat. This kind of approach will have a positive impact on lowering blood sugar levels and decreasing the risk of diabetes.

Alcohol

Refined alcohol is filled with sugar and empty calories without providing nutritional value, so it's not included in the Paleo diet.

Wine has a low alcohol content and is antioxidants rich. Even if it's not recommended, it can be considered as a "better" option.

Processed foods

First, you should forget the fast food. Say no to frozen meals. Don't buy sweets and snacks!

Grains

Paleo is a pre-agricultural diet. Grains (breads, pasta, rice, oats, and barley) are agricultural products and are not included in the Paleo diet. This products are high in carbohydrates.

Legumes

As with grains, legumes are agricultural products and are off-limits. This includes beans, lentils, peas, soy and soy products.

What to put on your Paleo plate?

Meats, eggs and seafood

Meats, eggs and seafood are the most important elements of the Paleo diet. This protein rich foods will give you the most of your calories. You can eat all meat (beef, lamb, pork, and poultry), fish, shellfish, mollusks and eggs from high quality sources. It's very important to be prepared with Paleo-friendly ingredients.

Healthy fats from plant sources

Extra virgin olive oil (made from the first cold pressing of the olives) is a great source of healthy fats rich in monounsaturated fatty acids. Coconut oil is also encouraged. Animal fats, butter and palm oil are also allowed.

Vegetables and fruits

Vegetables, especially leafy greens are very important in the Paleo diet and can be eaten in unlimited quantities. Fruits are allowed in limited quantities because of their high sugar content. Some great foraged fruits are berries, such as raspberries, cranberries, blueberries and strawberries. Tree fruits shouldn't be neglected: apples, pears, peaches, plums, nectarines, cherries and citrus fruits.

Beverages

Your main drink should be water. Natural fruit and vegetable juices are allowed but should be unsweetened and in limited quantities. Tea and coffee is fine (unsweetened and without dairy milk).

Condiments

It's best to rely on herbs and spices because condiments often contains sugar and other forbidden ingredients. For example ketchup is not allowed. Mustard is allowed only if it does not contain sugar.

STANDARD U.S./METRIC MEASURE-MENT CONVERSIONS

VOLUME CONVERSIONS	
U.S. Volume	Metric Equivalent
1/8 teaspoon	0.5 milliliter
1/4 teaspoon	1 milliliter
1/2 teaspoon	2 milliliters
1 teaspoon	5 milliliters
1/2 tablespoon	7 milliliters
1 tablespoon (3 teaspoons)	15 milliliters
2 tablespoons (1 fluid ounce)	30 milliliters
1/4 cup (4 tablespoons)	60 milliliters
1/3 cup	90 milliliters
1/2 cup (4 fluid ounces)	125 milliliters
2/3 cup	160 milliliters
3/4 cup (6 fluid ounces)	180 milliliters

VOLUME CONVERSIONS

U.S. Volume	Metric Equivalent
1 cup (16 tablespoons)	250 milliliters
1 pint (2 cups)	500 milliliters
1 quart (4 cups)	1 liter (about)

WEIGHT CONVERSIONS

U.S. Weight	Metric Equivalent
1/2 ounce	15 grams
1 ounce	30 grams
2 ounces	60 grams
3 ounces	85 grams
1/4 pound (4 ounces)	115 grams
1/2 pound (8 ounces)	225 grams
3/4 pound (12 ounces)	340 grams
1 pound (16 ounces)	454 grams

OVEN TEMPERATURE CONVERSIONS

Degrees Fahrenheit	Degrees Celsius
200 degrees F	95 degrees C
250 degrees F	120 degrees C
275 degrees F	135 degrees C
300 degrees F	150 degrees C
325 degrees F	160 degrees C
350 degrees F	180 degrees C
375 degrees F	190 degrees C
400 degrees F	205 degrees C
425 degrees F	220 degrees C
450 degrees F	230 degrees C